2015

Published by WSI (Words Sounds and Images)

ISBN numbers—

13: 978-1515326885

10: 1515326888

Visit the author at—

Website: www.kmkaung.com

Blog: http://kyimaykaung.blogspot.com

Facebook: www.facebook.com/kyi.m.kaung

Twitter: https://twitter.com/KyiKaung

Also by K.M.Kaung

Novellas:

Black Rice

ISBN-13: 978-0615797526

ISBN-10: 0615797520

The Lovers

ISBN-13:978-1499193725

ISBN 10-1499193726

The Rider of Crocodiles

ISBN-13:978-1497498365

ISBN 10: 1497498368

FGM

ISBN-13: 978-1497497733

ISBN-10: 1497497736

Dancing like a Peacock & Koel Bird

ISBN-13: 978-1497514850

ISBN-10: 1497514851

No Crib for a Bed and Other Stories

ISBN-13: 9781499200751

ISBN—10:

Novel:

Wolf—upcoming

Poetry:

Pelted with Petals: The Burmese Poems

Intertext, AK, 1996

ISBN: 0-912767-15-4

Tibetan Tanka

Intertext, AK, 1996

ISBN: 0-912767-14-6

Words Sounds & Images

Kyi May Kaung

[THE BEACH ANOMIE]

A Photo Essay

Dedication—

In memory of my father Sithu U Kaung, who taught me to observe carefully.

For my grandchildren, may you see but not too much.

Anomie

1. Social instability

   Instability caused by the erosion or abandonment of moral and social

   codes

2. Social alienation

   A feeling of disorientation and alienation from society caused by the

   perceived absence of a supporting social or moral framework.

   Encarta Dictionary: English (North America)

   7-29-2015

CV OF THE PHOTOGRAPHER/AUTHOR.

KYI MAY KAUNG (PH.D.)

Curriculum Vitae

Website: www.kmkaung.com

Blog http://kyimaykaung.blogspot.com

Objective: Seeking teaching, writing/research or advocacy position. Available for international conferences, seminars and private consultancy.

- Passionately interested in Burma and democracy/social justice, human rights, women's and children's issues.

- Fifteen years of non-profit experience in the Washington, DC area.

- Able to strategize and set up new organizations.

- Able to speak and write persuasively so people listen.

- Excellent oral and written presentations. Convincing, engaging and experienced public speaker. Fluent English and Burmese. Reading knowledge of French. Willing to learn Mandarin.

- Extensive contacts in academia, politics and the arts.

- Strengths: Very fast and efficient researcher – Lexus-Nexus etc. on line.

- Fast and accurate boil down of important issues to easily understandable points.

- Political Economy of Asia: Asean countries, India and China, Burma specialist.

- Able to travel internationally up to 25% of the year.

- Able to formulate strategy and analyze organizational structure and goals.

- Able to formulate and carry out P.R. initiatives.

EDUCATION

Ph.D. City and Regional Planning and Political Science, University of Pennsylvania, May 1994.

M.A. City and Regional Planning, University of Pennsylvania, 1987.

M.A. Economics, University of Rangoon, 1967.

B.A. Honors, Economics, University of Rangoon, 1964.

DISSERTATION

"Modernization, Breakdown and Structural Configurations: Retrogression in Burma (1962-1992)."

Chairman: Henry Teune, Political Science, University of Pennsylvania.

Members: Josef Silverstein, Professor Emeritus, Rutgers University.

Donald E. Smith, Political Science, University of Pennsylvania.

Seymour Mandelbaum, City Planning, University of Pennsylvania

INTERVIEWED BY:

Khin May Zaw of 7 Day Journal about publishing electronically, 2-25-2014, in Burmese.

Khin May Zaw of 7 Day Journal about World Economic Forum and foreign direct investment in Burma – 6-10-2013

https://www.facebook.com/photo.php?fbid=393254867462748&set=a.2682 75419960694.63683.268229929965243&type=1&theater

Patrick Barta of Wall Street Journal – Oct 2012, about Rangoon University before the 1962 coup.

Michelle Chen of Asia Pacific Forum interviewed me about change in Burma, is it real. Dec 13th, 2011 http://www.asiapacificforum.org/show-detail.php?show_id=250

October 2011 Kyaw Aung Lwin of VOA interviewed me about poetry reading in front of Burmese embassy DC – 10,000 poets for change.

Kyaw Aung Lwin, VOA on my participation in Poetry Walk of Shame.

White Dove Women's Journal, Chiangmai, Thailand, 2009 on 2010 election in Burma.

September 2009, interviewed for video of my art show Mostly Burmese Monks, by VOA Burmese section.

http://www.youtube.com/watch?v=UvlXLXpQP8E

RFA Feb. 14, 2009 Kyaw Min Htun – Beacon Art Show in honor of Aung San Suu Kyi, panelist.

Jan 1, 2008 RFA, "Burma's Economic Prospects in 2008."

September 2007 Burmese Monks' Crisis

1. BBC (World) HardTalk --

http://news.bbc.co.uk/2/hi/programmes/hardtalk/7026645.stm

2. KALW San Francisco Radio – Your Call with Rose Aguiler

http://yourcallradio.blogspot.com/

3. CBC – with Suhana Meharchand in Toronto –

Sept. 24th, 2007 – in which I correctly predicted that the clampdown would happen in the next 24 hours.

October 4, 2007 – post-clampdown analysis –

4. Ask Hugh (Williamson) – radio out of Berkeley, CA.

5. CapeTown Voice – Jihad Omar – On Burmese Monks' Saffron Revolution.

2001- 2007:

Canadian Broadcasting Corporation; National Public Radio; Voice of America Burmese Service and Talk to America; Pacifica Radio; Radio Free Asia; Asian Fortune (Ying Ju Lai); Dr. Michael Hurd Show; Montgomery County TV. Art Scene Channel 16 Lila Snow, Artist; Gazette Newspaper (Audrey Dutton); Silver Spring MD Impact Awards; Boulder Alternative Radio; Kalamazoo Gazette; Boulder Current; Wild River Review; Anil Mundra; Eliot Pfanstiehl.

CITED IN:

Khin May Zaw – Foreign Direct Investment in Burma and World Economic Forum (in Burmese) in 7 Day Journal 6-11-2013

https://www.facebook.com/photo.php?fbid=393254867462748&set=a.2632 75419960694.63683.268229929965243&type=1&theater

"We are on the rebound with Obama" by Mulindwa Edwards, Foreign Policy in Focus. Web accessed 4-109

http://www.mail-archive.com/ugandanet@kym.net/msg26224.html

LATEST PUBLICATIONS AND PRESENTATIONS

A review of James Michener's Recessional-1-5-2013

http://www.amazon.com/Recessional-Novel-James-A-Michener/product-reviews/0449223450/ref=cm_cr_dp_see_all_btm?ie=UTF8&showViewpoints=1&sortBy=bySubmissionDateDescending

A review of contemporary Burmese poetry –

http://www.englishpen.org/wp-content/uploads/2012/04/From-the-Archive-of-Censored-Materials-report.pdf

July, 2013, edited by ko ko thett for English PEN

In process – co-editing book on Rohingya in Burma with Dr. Paul Chambers, Payap University, Chiangmai, Thailand.

Published my poem Vultures over Burma in Foreign Policy in Focus

June 2013

http://www.fpif.org/articles/vultures_over_burma

Published my novella Black Rice in Kindle and print format on Amazon

May 2013

http://www.amazon.com/Black-Rice-Novella-K-Kaung/dp/0615797520

Member, Round Table on Ethnic Conflict in Burma and "Change"

Low Library, Columbia Univ. NY – AK Sen was the keynote speaker.

I suggested and helped invite four round table participants, who are specialists on the Rohingya Muslims of Burma.

2012 Asian Correspondent

http://asiancorrespondent.com/75742/burma-economists-generals-and-culture-vultures/

Himal Southasia – 2012, short story Black Belt.

Dec 2011, special Burma issue, Himal Southasia, Potemkin Politics: Are Burmese reforms for real.

http://himalmag.com/component/authors/articles/Kyi-May-Kaung.html

Oct 24, 2011. Poetry reading in front of Burmese embassy DC on PeacexPeace.

Oct 14, 2011 – on Asian Correspondent –

http://asiancorrespondent.com/67276/zarganar-or-pincers-great-burmese-comic-among-few-released/

Mentioned in Sarah Browning's article on Poetry Walk of Shame in Foreign Policy in Focus.

http://www.fpif.org/articles/poets_stand_up

Oct 12, 2011. Poem War Against Roaches in Foreign Policy in Focus.

http://www.fpif.org/articles/war_on_roaches

Sept 24, 2011. Featured poet – reading in front of Burmese embassy DC etc. Poetry Walk of Shame, sponsored by Institute of Policy Studies and Spilt This Rock.

Interviewed by VOA etc. VOA interview broadcast to Burma.

Sept. 9. 2011 Poem - War on Roaches, in Counterpunch

http://www.counterpunch.org/2011/09/09/jared-carter-and-kyi-may-kaung/

Oct 28, 2010. How the Burmese junta tried to fool the world with sham elections.

Payap University, Chiangmai, Thailand, co-presenter with Win Min.

Oct 16, 2010, 7-10 PM, on SULU DC Asian American poets – the Dome at the Artisphere, Rosslyn, VA.

September 2010, Open Salon, book reviews of JoAnne Growney, Red has no Reason, poetry collection,

Mischa Berlinski's novel Fieldwork, and

William Dalrymple's The last Mughul, history. Book reviews.

Napalm Health Spa, Summer 2010. My poem Loss.

https://www.poetspath.com/napalm/nhs10/index.html

Praised by Native American poet Susan Deer Cloud.

Book review of Win Tin, What's That? A Human Hell, in Foreign Policy in Focus and Truthout, Eurasian Review etc.

http://www.truth-out.org/a-review-u-win-tin-whats-that-a-human-hell-in-burmese58707

http://www.ips-dc.org/articles/review_whats_that_a_human_hell

Summer 2009, short story No Crib for a Bed, in anthology of DC women writers, Gravity Dancers, edited by Richard Peabody –

http://www.amazon.com/Gravity-Dancers-Fiction-Washington-Women/dp/0931181305

The Northern Virginia Review. March 26, 2009. Reception launch of Issue 23, which includes my short story, "53 Red Roses." David Baldacci, guest speaker.

National Coalition Government of the Union of Burma. Confidential Report. "A Democratic Vision for Burma: How to turn Burma Around." Dec. 08-March 30, 2009.

Comments in Irrawaddy on line on "Burmese democracy movement has no vision"

http://www.irrawaddymedia.com/opinion_story.php?art_id=15229

Art display – "Burmese Mugs" Portraits and "Memory Rolls." American University Library/US Campaign for Burma, Washington DC, March 2009.

Short Story – 53 Red Roses, in The Northern Virginia Review, #23, March 2009.

http://www.nvcc.edu/depts/nvreview/nvr-latest.htm

International Art Awareness Drive for Aung San Suu Kyi. Mirca/Beacon Art, panelist, Feb. 14, 2009. Interviewed by RFA.

http://www.mizzima.com/news/world/1689-international-artists-launch-awareness-drive-for-aung-san-suu-kyi.html

Institute of Policy Studies, Panelist – War, Memory and Representation in Art, Georgetown, Washington DC. Dec. 2008. http://www.ips-dc.org/events/1008

Foreign Policy in Focus – "War and Peace" article on Vietnamese artist Huong.

FPIF, Book review of Joseph Stigltiz and Linda Bilmes' The Three Trillion Dollar War.

Counterpunch – poem "Burma at a Critical Juncture." Dec. 12, 2008.

http://www.counterpunch.org/poems12262008.html

Panel discussions: Burma and India, 60 years after Independence. April 2, 2008

Prospects for Peace and Democracy in Burma, April 3, 2008 – NEIU, Chicago, 13th Annual Asian American Festival.

"All about Cambodia" A literature survey type discussion on books about Cambodia. Dr. Kaung's Bookshelf, March 28, 2008, Silver Spring, MD.

Burma: Post Clampdown, What should be done? Presentation at Payap University, Chiangmai, Thailand, Feb. 25, 2008.

Burma: Monks and Democracy, Jan. 24, 2008. Woman's National Democratic Club, Washington DC. (Oral presentation)

War and Peace, an epic mural – The art of Vietnamese artist Huong.

http://www.art2all.net/tranh/huong/huong_peacemural.html

Special three-part program on Economic Prospects for Burma, China and India in 2008. Jan 2008. Interviewed by Khin May Zaw of RFA. (This program was praised by economists inside Burma)

Burma: Post Clampdown – What Should be Done? The American Prospect, on line. October 2007.

Burma: Prospects for Social Activism, Oct. 17, 2007. American University, SIS Lounge. With Steven Hansch and Mike Haack.

United States Senate Hearing of Oct. 2, 2007. New Mandala, a publication of Australian National University.

Also on my blog – http://kyimaykaung.blogspot.com

(Oral presentation – International Development Program Student Association, American University – Oct 19, 2007)

In house policy briefs for VAHU Development Institute.

How to Find out the Truth about Burma, paper on primary sources with respect to current crisis. New Mandala (A Publication of Australian National University), Nov. 2007.

October http://kyimaykaung.blogspot.com

Foreign Policy in Focus, Monks vs The Military, Sept. 26, 2007, http://www.fpif.org/fpiftxt/4582

Foreign Policy in Focus, Burma, Growing Darker Daily, 9-11-2007 – on current crisis in Burma.

FPIF, "Out of Burma" (on Burmese literature) July 13, 2007.

http://www.fpif.org/fpiftxt/4374

A mention on International Exchange for Poetic Invention--Thank you Linh Dinh☐

http://poeticinvention.blogspot.com/2007/03/kyi-may-kaung.html

NEIU – Chicago, In Honor of Aung San Suu Kyi, panelist, April 2007.

http://www.afsc.org/ht/display/EventDetails/i/54289/pid/16705

Foreign Policy in Focus, Out of Burma- on dissident literature in Burma.

Asian Fortune, Obit of U Kyaw Htun, Washington Times Editor.

Asian Fortune, on Vineeta Gupta, Indian AIDS activist.

Asian Fortune Newspaper. May 2007. Articles on Bob James' Jazz and Angels of Shanghai,

On Hla Ohn Mae, Burmese dissident. www.asianfortune.com

Foreign Policy in Focus. Debate on Sanctions in Burma. Jan. 2007

Wild River Review Blog, Reflections on a Begging Bowl: Monks Demonstrate in Burma. Sept 26, 2007.

Wild River Review – Burmese Migrant Workers and Shrimp Shelling and Tuna Canning in Mahachai, Thailand – March14, 2007.

Also in Burma Economic Watch, on line.

OpenDemocracy articles. 2006-2007

"Bank Crisis Reeks of a Ponzi Scheme, Feb. 2003, Irrawaddy on line.

http://www.irrawaddy.org/opinion_story.php?art_id=342

The Irrawaddy (Burmese dissident magazine – read by members of Congress)

Sept 2001 "Ms Ma Thanegi's Rules of Good Political Etiquette"
http://216.104.44.206/opinion_story.php?art_id=251&page=1

Launched Nov. 2, 2007 – Dr. Kaung's Book Shelf – a series of book discussions – at Space 710, Silver Spring, MD. Currently on leave.

Wild River Review- fiction – short story The Lovers

http://www.wildriverreview.com/2/2-shortstories_lovers.html

Burma Economic Watch – Macquarie Univ, Sydney, Australia,

http://www.businessandeconomics.mq.edu.au/our_departments/Economics/Econ_docs/bew/2006/2006_Shrimp_Shelling_and_Tuna_Canning.pdf

Co-founded – VAHU Development Institute, a think tank without walls, for Burma, 2005. Over the recent Burma crisis, VAHU analysts were interviewed a total of 120 times. We have trained 60 monks and 90 civilian non-profit workers in batches.

Musica Viva poetry performance – writeup. Oct 23, 2005.

http://www.dcmusicaviva.org/documents/alenier_102305.pdf

From 2004, my poem inspired by Neruda, Love Poem appeared here in CD form.

http://www.amazon.com/rattapallax-Marjorie-Marciano-Nicomedes-Suarez-Arauz/dp/B00F6QXGRC

Jan. 6th 2003, Chiangmai, Thailand, International Association for the Study of Forced Migration. Forced migration on the Burma-Thai border: Why they are here and the search for humane solutions.

Sept. 2002. Gothenburg, Sweden. Burma Studies.

Diplomacy: the Nature of Dialogue and Reconciliation. Coordinator with David Steinberg. Panelists, Dr Zarni, Zaw Oo, Dr. Chao Tzang Yawngwe, Aung Zaw of Irrawaddy (Steinberg did not allow him on panel), U Thet Tun (statistician and former diplomat, from inside Burma), Morton Pedersen.

Flux, joint art exhibition with Henry Callahan, Foundry Gallery, Dupont Circle, Washington DC.

http://www.henrycallahan.com/press/

Theories, Paradigms or Models in Burma Studies, Asian Survey, 1995.

Excerpt from my allegory, She-Monkey goes West, The Golden Time, in CrossConnect, 1995

http://ccat.sas.upenn.edu/xconnect/volume1/issue2/word/fiction.html

AWARDS AND HONORS

April 2012, Northeastern Illinois University, Award for my contributions to Asian-American Festival, Chicago.

Since 2009, contributing member, Free Aung San Suu Kyi and Burma website.

Northeastern Illinois University, Distinguished Service Award, for Outstanding Dedication and Work promoting Peace and Democracy in Burma, April 3, 2008.

IMPACTSilverSpring Award, won by Space 7-10 where my Dr. Kaung's Salon is located.   2007

Short List – Earth Rights International PR position 2005 based in Chiangmai, Thailand.

Best short story "Black Rice" and best art entry – Painting Mars Ranger – March 2007, The Northern Virginia Review.

William Carlos Williams Award, Academy of American Poets, 1995.

Pennsylvania Council on the Arts Award, for concept for play FLASHBACK (now titled Shaman.)

Pew Finalist, 1996 and 1994, for play SHAMAN and allegory She-Monkey respectively.

Fulbright Scholar, 1982-89. University of Pennsylvania.

Polish-Burma Exchange Scholar, 1969-70. Central School of Economics and Statistics, Warsaw, Poland. First place winner.

M.A. with distinction, first in class, Rangoon, 1967.

B.A. first division, first place winner, 1964.

VOLUNTEER POSITIONS

Supporter – U.S. Campaign for Burma.

Co-founder, founding board member – VAHU. A think tank without walls for Burma.

Founder/facilitator/presenter: Dr. Kaung's Salon and Dr. Kaung's Bookshelf, 963 Bonifant St. Silver Spring, MD.

Dr. Kaung's Salon from Oct 2005-present – some selected topics: Pakistan and the Benazir Bhutto. Monologue as a hysterectomy victim. Book discussion --

Beasts of No Nation, by Uzodinma Iweala. Robin Hood Ballads by Dr. Stephen Winick, Discussion of Nobel prize winning writer Orhan Pamuk, James Frey's A Million Little Pieces, book launches by artist Lila Snow, journalist Melissa Robinson, architect Werner Krebs on stage design, Eniko Basa on The 1956 Hungarian Revolution, dancers Martha Wittman and Elizabeth Johnson choreographing immigrant stories, Elizabeth Null folk sing, Christmas Carol Sing, Bijan C. Bayne and Tomiko Anders on "Who am I?" My wearable art show, dancer Gretchen Dunn performing placeDISplace, , Meena Nayak Endless Rain, book launch.

Member, FBB – Friday Brunch Group – networking for writers with Nita Congress, August 2007-

Co-founder, Member, Writing Group, WRITE ON, DC. August 2005 – Sept. 2006

Co-founder, Writing Group, The East-West Group, MD, April 2005 - Oct 2005

Member, Washington Independent Writers, Travel Writers' Group, 2006-

Board member, Burma Refugee Project, (medical aid to refugees), Jan 2005-present

Board Member, Burma Economic Watch, An Electronic Magazine, Macquarie University, Sydney, Australia. 2004 to present.

Member, Technical Advisory Network, Burmese Government in Exile, 2000-present.

ART EXHIBITIONS

Flux - Foundry Gallery, Dupont Circle, DC, 2001

http://www.washingtoncitypaper.com/articles/23599/henry-callahan-kyi-may-kaung

Mostly Burmese Blotches, Space 7-10, Silver Spring, MD 2005

Yo Franz, Yo Jackson, abstract expressionist paintings, Suvarnabhuni Gallerr, Chiangmai, Thailand, 2006.

http://www.goldentriangleart.com/2007/06/art-exhibitions.html

Mostly Burmese Mugs, Space 7-10, Silver Spring, MD 2007.

http://ww2.gazette.net/stories/032107/bethnew231523_32328.shtml

Mostly Burmese Monks, Ubud, Bali, March 2008.

Human Rights portraits, American University, 2008.

Human Rights Portraits, Hotel Arthur, Helsinki, Finland, 2008.

Abstracts, Payap University, Chiangmai, Thailand, 2008.

Mostly Burmese Monks, Space 7-10, MD 2009

http://pinklineproject.com/event/167

Cut and Paste, Collages, Friendship Heights Village Center, 2009.

Cut and Paste, Collages, Suiriya Gallery, Chiangmai, Thailand, 2008.

WORK

International Diplomat, Program Officer, December 2008- May 2009.

Private Consultant – 2004-

2006- VAHU co-founder and Sr. Analyst.

2005- Consultant and Free Lance Writer. Professional artist.

Senior Research Associate. The Burma Fund, Washington DC, Sept 2001-Dec 31, 2004

Senior Research Analyst. Radio Free Asia, Washington DC, May 1998-Sept 2001.

International Radio Broadcaster, RFA Burmese Service, Washington DC, March 1997-April 1998.

1982-1994. Ph.D. candidate, University of Pennsylvania, Philadelphia.

1978-1988. Assoc. Professor, Economics Department, University of Rangoon, Burma.

RESEARCH INTERESTS/WORK IN PROGRESS

The Rohingya Issue and Race in Burma.

Burma, the sham elections of 2010 and 2015.

Burma – Transition to Democracy, A Strategic Action Plan, commissioned paper for The Burmese Democratic Government in Exile, Dec.1 2008 - June30, 2009.

China, India, Thailand and Burma and ASEAN, USA.

United States Political Economy

Effects of Global Warming.

Greater Mekong Region, environmental problems.

Yangtze Dams.

Dissertation to Book --- completed August 2004. Nordic Institute of Asian Studies Press, Copenhagen.

Economic Transitions in Burma: Strategies and Scenarios. Book length project, co-authored with Zaw Oo, The Burma Fund, 2002.

•   About possible scenarios should there be democratic change and the World Bank and IMF enter Burma. I intensively studied Joseph Stiglitz' points of criticism.

Migration on Thai-Burma Border, Thai policies and SPDC Roadmap.

SPDC Roadmap and Problems.

2004 – Second Wholesale Sell Off of Natural Resources in Burma.

2004 –2007 Sanctions vs. No Sanctions: United States' Burma Policy.

•   Human rights, especially women's and children's rights.

•   Closed vs. open systems.

•   Command economies vs. open markets.

•   IMF and World Bank packages and shortcomings.

•   US policy and Burma, the Burmese democracy movement,

•   System change and democratic, market reforms in China and Russia etc.

•   Causes and effects of out-migration and search for humane solutions.

•   Burma and Asean, community of democracies.

•   Alternative models and their application to Burma.

•   Problems of transition in Burma, Vietnam, Russia, Poland.

•   Chinese Economic Reforms 1978-present, N and S Korea.

- Exploring humane solutions to Thai-Burma refugee problem.

Economic History. J.S. Furnivall and Economic Planning, the Plural Society in Burma during the U Nu (democratic) period in Burma 1948-62.

Novel in Progress, about a Burmese dissident.

Collection of Short Stories.

Play development -- Shaman

Painting – abstracts and iconic figures – 3 one woman shows in greater DC area since 2001, shows in Chiangmai, Thailand, July 2007 and Feb. 2008.

SEMINARS/CONFERENCES, STRATEGIZING SESSIONS 2001 –

Jan. 24, 2008. Strategizing meeting for Burma activism. Woman's National Demcratic Club, D.C.

Oct 19, 2007. Panelist. Burma- Post Clampdown, What is to be Done? American University, School of International Studies.

April 27, 2007. Panelist on Education and Generational Change. Burma Youth Project, American University, Washington, DC.

April 22, 2007 my arts and craft show at Mayorga Coffee Factory, sponsored by American University, International Rescue Committee.

April 5, 2007, Northeastern Illinois University, Focus on Burma and Aung San Suu Kyi – On the keynote panel.

Dec. 2006, Chiangmai University, Community Development Project. Read course attendees project paper proposals and chose winning team.

November 2006, Refugee Conference – American University – one of invited speakers.

October- Dec., 2006. Refugee art exhibit, one of invited painters. Helped plan the exhibition, Gateway Heliport Gallery, Silver Spring, MD.

July 2006, E-W Center DC sponsored a closed door conference on Conflict Resolution in Burma in Bangkok. I was one of a dozen invited commentators/rapporteurs.

July 2006, Burma Studies Group – Singapore.

2005- Co-founder, founding board member (with Zaw Oo) of VAHU which trains non-profit workers from Burma.

October 2005, The Politics of Voices, House of World Culture, Berlin. Invited with 5 other S.E. Asian writers "who dare to confront."

October 2004. Panel on Burma, "The Latest Purge in Burma," Burma Studies Center, DeKalb IL. Keynote Panelist.

September 2004, Bank Information Center, Open Society Institute. Washington DC

- Helped plan seminar on World Bank and IMF, Lessons from Bosnia, suggested Joseph Stiglitz be invited, worked on my mentor Ronald Findlay of Columbia University Economics department being there to introduce Stiglitz, liaised with and introduced three economists from Burma. OSI funding.

March 2004. Closed door strategizing session on Burma, SAIS Johns Hopkins, Washington DC.

March 2004, The Burma Fund, Young Scholars Forum at American University, Washington DC. Paper proposals of Burma scholars in USA and discussions on research methodology

August-September 2003, Research on G.H. Luce and Furnivall Archives.

July 2003, helped formulate interview questions for Migrant Workers Survey on Thai-Burma Border (collaborative project with Macquarie University, Sydney, Australia.

Jan 2003 International Association for Study of Forced Migration, paper on Burmese refugees, Thailand and SPDC "roadmap."

March 2002 Technical Advisory Network, NCGUB, Bangkok, Thailand. Role of Advisors of Burmese Government in Exile.

Nov. 2002. SAIS, Johns Hopkins, Washington DC. Participant. Strategizing for Burmese democracy movement in exile.

Sept, 2002. Burma Studies Conference, Gottenberg, Sweden, co-chaired panel on Diplomacy and Dialog in Burma.

Jan 2003, Conference on Forced Migration and Burma, Chiengmai, Thailand.

July 2003, Canberra, Australia, Australian National University, Peer Reviewed book on Economic Transitions in Burma. Peers from Burmese Democratic Government in Exile,

July 2003, Sydney, Australia, Australia Burmese Students Conference.

March 2003, Globalization and Human Trafficking, Denver CO.

Aug. 2002, International IDEA Stockholm, Democratic Capacity Building for Burma.

August 2002, Asean People's Assembly, "Globalisation and ASEAN," Bali, Indonesia.

April 2001 Conference on World Affairs, Boulder CO. "World without Borders."

*

www.ingramcontent.com/pod-product-compliance
Lightning Source LLC
Chambersburg PA
CBHW041508280526
45792CB00004B/1172